Poka Yoke - Design for Great Quality

Mohammed Hamed Ahmed Soliman

Published by personal-lean.org, 2023.

POKA YOKE - DESIGN FOR GREAT QUALITY

First edition. November 5, 2023.

Table of Contents

Dedication

I created this book with the help of many different business resources. These academic articles and books are all cited at the end of this book. A number of people have influenced my learning journey and my entire career. I would like to acknowledge them here.

Esraa Soliman: My lovely wife and partner. She encouraged me to write and publish this work. In fact, she always encourages me to do creative work.

Jeffrey Liker: Professor at the University of Michigan and author of *The Toyota Way* and the amazing Toyota series of books. His impressive work on Toyota inspired and influenced my learning about the Toyota Production System. I would really like to thank him for his indirect involvement in this work. Many examples included in this book were originally from his books. Although I have never met Jeff face to face, we have had great communications over social media platforms.

Chris Duklet: A lean manufacturing leader from the United States who works in the field of health care. He has contributed to this work by reviewing the book prior to publication and giving me useful recommendations and advice.

Attia Gomaa: Professor at the American University in Cairo who influenced my teaching career at the university and taught me how to become a good trainer.

Steven Borris: A business consultant, author, and friend from England who influenced my writing career. He encouraged me to write and publish. Steven was my mentor on lean manufacturing, helping me first to understand the basics, after which I developed my understanding through deep practice and self-directed learning.

Eslam Soliman: My friend and a professor at the Assiut University. His PhD is from the University of New Mexico. He has influenced my entire writing career by giving me recommendations and advice on how to write and publish. He revised my published works many times and kept inspiring me after every piece I wrote and published.ng.

Poka Yoke- Design for Great Quality
Toyota Production System Concepts

Poka-yoke is a Japanese term used at Toyota that means making something so it can't be done incorrectly. If you don't know about it, that's alright. Most people I know who are not connected to Toyota have never heard of this term. It's basically a way to make things idiot-proof. The term used to be offensive, so it was changed. But in your everyday life, you will encounter poka-yoke without even knowing it. Have you ever accidentally pressed the open button on your running microwave and noticed it turned off? That's called poka-yoke. Instead of making you turn off the microwave yourself before opening the door, the safety switch automatically stops the power so you won't get exposed to radiation if you make a mistake. If you've ever connected something to a USB port, you have used poka-yoke. Do you see how you can't plug it in the wrong way? That's because it was made that way on purpose to avoid putting it in the wrong way.

Historical background

Have you ever asked yourself why Japanese cars are famous for being dependable? You can still find Japanese cars that are 20 years old running smoothly alongside the newest and best cars in the automotive industry. That's why they keep their worth so good for all these years. Just search online for the prices of used Toyota Camry and Chevrolet Malibu cars that are 10 years old. Toyota became successful as a car company in the 20th century because of a new way they made their cars called the Toyota Production System. After that, Toyota became famous in the car industry for making really good and strong vehicles that rarely have problems, unlike other companies. The TPS led the way for many of the efficient manufacturing methods used by other industries today.

The Toyota Production System was created by Taiichi Ohno and Eiji Toyoda from 1948 to 1975. This text is about 7 types of waste in manufacturing. These wastes are overproduction, idle time, transportation, the manufacturing process itself, excess stock, unnecessary movement, and defects.

In the 1960s, a Toyota engineer named Shigeo Shingo wanted to get rid of the problem of mistakes. He saw that workers sometimes forgot to put the right springs under the button, and this caused a problem. Because of that, he changed the way the parts were put together. Now, the first step is for the workers to get the springs ready by putting them in a special spot. Then, they can put the springs into the switch. When a spring was left in the wrong place, workers noticed the error and fixed it easily before adding more springs.

Shingo came up with a solution that was both simple and clever. He understood that people would make mistakes and that mistakes were the reasons for problems. So, he decided that it was better to stop mistakes from happening in the beginning instead of correcting them later. He named this solution a poka-yoke.

Fixing things that are broken is a waste of time and effort.

If we think about it, when we start, everything is in a good condition. Then you accidentally make a mistake. It's bound to happen unless you're a robot. Sometimes, we don't realize a mistake until the customer receives a faulty product and complains about it. First, you will ask people to return the product. You will pay for the shipping to make the returns easier. Then, you will disassemble the product and repair any issues. After that, the product will be returned to its original and functional condition. Looking at it from a simple point of view, creating a mistake, finding it, and correcting it (or getting rid of it) is a waste of time because it doesn't add any extra value. You have to start all over again, even though you worked really hard.

Making mistakes is something that all people do.

error-proofing) measures This means putting systems and procedures in place to prevent mistakes from occurring or catching them before they cause significant harm. By acknowledging the inevitability of mistakes and taking measures to mitigate their impact, we can create a more reliable and efficient environment. Poka-yoke is a way to prevent mistakes or errors from happening. Finding the origin or cause usually involves asking a sequence of "why" questions.

Stop Errors from Happening in the Beginning.

Poka-yoke is a system that stops mistakes and tells the user if mistakes have happened. If your product is made of physical parts, you can limit what it can do. Make use of different shapes and create a situation where it is impossible for the user to make mistakes.

Designing Poka-Yoke in Your Products

Designing poka-yoke in your products refers to incorporating mistake-proofing techniques that prevent errors or defects from occurring.

So, how does this work in design. It's simpler to say create a product that stops users from making mistakes, but I think it's more complicated than that. Let's talk about something that we often do on a website: filling out forms. Imagine we made a form that allows users to fill in their payment details. If we didn't have any poka-yoke, the system would not stop the user from making errors. If someone made a mistake while entering their credit card or phone number, the system would save that mistake without realizing it until it attempted to process the information or someone tried to contact them by phone.

A poka-yoke is like a checker that makes sure the information you enter is correct before allowing you to submit it. But I think this is not sufficient. Errors were still made. We found the mistake and informed the user, so they could fix it. What we want is to stop mistakes from happening in the beginning. For example, use a tool to sort or sift through something.

Poka-yoke Methods Primarily Concentrate on Making Improvements to Processes.

Toyota is really good at making sure all its team members understand and follow their TPS methodologies. They make sure this becomes a natural part of how they work. I remember when I attended a meeting for new employees. We learned about the main ideas of the Toyota Production System. They told us about Kaizen, which means always trying to make things better. It encourages Team Members to come up with new and creative ways to improve how we do things. Actually, TPS was not created suddenly. This means that from the late 1940's to the mid-70's, processes were repeated and improved continuously, and most of the elements that we have today were put into action during that time.

There are many instances of Poka-Yoke in our daily routines.

There are large number of applications in real world regarding the use of mistake proofing in product design. Examples: Limit switches to assure a part correctly placed or fixture before process is performed; part features that only allow assembly the correct way, unique connectors to avoid misconnecting wire harnesses or cables, part symmetry that avoids incorrect insertion.

1. " Car safety features are designed to protect passengers and reduce the likelihood of accidents.

Cars have many safety features to prevent mistakes and keep us safe while driving. If you leave the car doors open or someone is sitting in the passenger seat without fastening their seatbelt, the car will beep or show a light. These are examples of alert functions that tell users about possible errors.

Safety technology has gotten a lot better in the past few years. Nowadays, lots of cars have sensors that tell drivers if they are moving out of their lane or getting too close to another car or object.

2. Treadmills

Treadmills are exercise machines that allow you to walk, jog, or run indoors and simulate the experience of walking or running outdoors.

Treadmills need to have a safety clip that, when pulled, stops the treadmill. This safety feature stops the treadmill if the person using it falls down (assuming they are wearing the clip) to keep them from getting hurt.

3. Microwaves, washing machines, dishwashers, and other appliances used in homes.

Some machines like microwaves, washing machines, dryers, and dishwashers won't work if their doors are open. specific set of criteria or circumstances) are met. These functions ensure that the process does not start until the necessary conditions are in place. All the requirements for closing the door have been fulfilled.

4. Elevators are machines that move people or things up and down in buildings. Garage doors are the big doors that open and close to let cars in and out of a garage.

Most elevators have sensors that stop the doors from closing if there is something or someone in the way. Garage doors, subway doors, and other automatic doors also have this feature. Some elevators make a beeping sound and stop working if there are too many people inside.

5. Spell-check functions are tools or features that automatically check the spelling of words in a document or text.

Spell-check is a way to find and fix mistakes when we write, but many people don't realize how important it is. Our phones, software, and internet browsers have tools that tell us if we make mistakes in spelling or grammar. They also sometimes fix the mistakes for us. This helps us not sound silly when we talk to others online. It's like a way to make sure we don't make mistakes.

6. Water bottles and travel mugs that don't leak.

Some cups and bottles need you to push and keep your finger on a button to take a sip from them. This mechanism stops the liquid from leaking or spilling out when the person is not using the cup to drink.

7. Power outlets are electrical sockets used to plug in devices that require electricity. USB plugs are a type of connector that allows devices to be connected and charged using a USB port.

Some plugs, like 3-pin and USB plugs, can only be put into the outlet in one way. This helps to prevent mistakes by using the shape of the plug.

8. Sink overflow outlets

Sink overflow outlets are holes in the sinks that allow excess water to drain out of the sink instead of overflowing onto the countertop.

Many sinks have a small opening near the pipe that stops water from spilling out if the drain gets clogged.

9. Lawnmower safety bars

Lawnmower safety bars are devices that help keep people safe while operating lawnmowers.

In the United States, lawnmowers must have a safety feature called a "deadman control" that needs to be activated for the blades to work. This control is usually a lever that is connected to the handle. The operator needs to press the lever for the lawnmower to start running.

10. Wheelchair wheels

Wheelchair wheels are the part of a wheelchair that help it move. They are circular and spin around to make the wheelchair go forward, backward, or turn.

The wheels on a wheelchair are made to stop moving when the chair is not being pushed. This makes sure that the person using the wheelchair doesn't slip while getting in or out of it, and doesn't get into a dangerous situation if the wheelchair starts moving without control.

Quality Improvement Techniques

There are many tools to accomplish the quality goals at every aspect of the process. There are many tools that will help prevent quality problems before they occur and allow you to plan for an error-free product. To assess a product failure and determine failure mechanism that need mistake-proofing you may need the use of a technique like failure mode and effect analysis.

Failure mode effect analysis (FMEA) is a process of assessing the failure risk based on its occurrence, severity, and detectability. The more detectable methods we have in the system to detect and predict failure, the lower the risk of the product failure. FMEA and if used properly, can be a good tool in improving quality. An article that I wrote and published in the Industrial Management magazine "Analyzing Failure to Prevent Problems" can illustrate this as well. Many organizations only use FMEA during the design stage, but FMEA can be really used in manufacturing, design, service and maintenance.

Poka Yoka which is a Japanese term, also refers to mistake-proofing is an effective tool to prevent human-errors. I have personally used it many times when conducting a failure mode effect analysis process. This tool can improve quality in many business processes include service, manufacturing, and design. Inventory control is another technique that is usually associated with any mistake proofing device.

Lean is not a toolkit for manufacturing to lower costs for profitability. Lean is a long-term strategy to satisfy customers through better quality and lower costs. Engineering a product that solve your customer's usage problems is a legitimate lean goal. Lean is about innovation and creativity. If you can manufacture defect-free product or build quality into the design, this will help satisfy customers and increase their confidence.

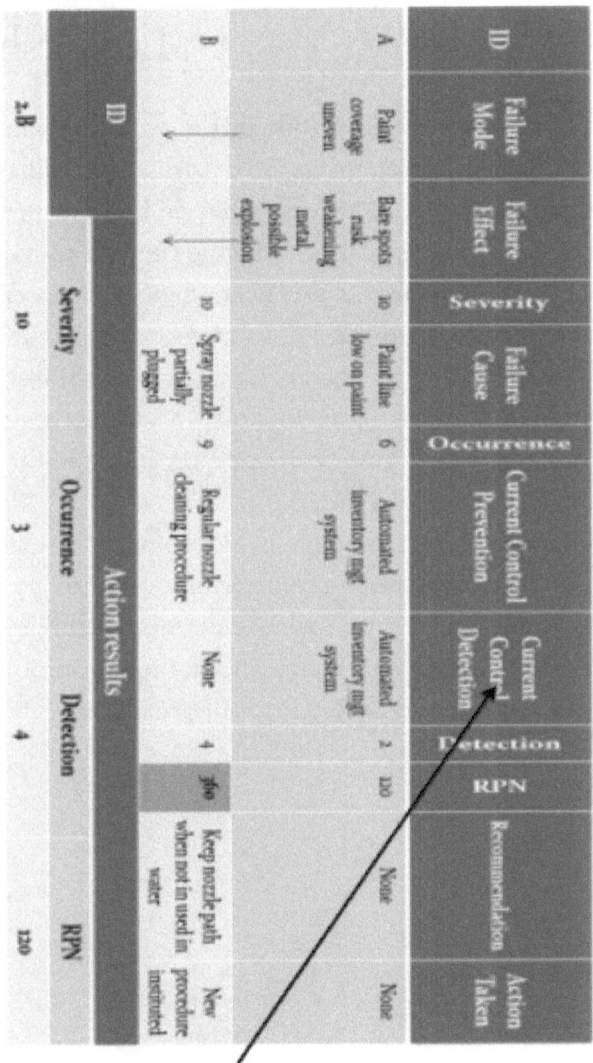

ID	Failure Mode	Failure Effect	Severity	Failure Cause	Occurrence	Current Control Prevention	Current Control Detection	Detection	RPN	Recommendation	Action Taken
A	Paint coverage uneven	Bare spots risk weakening metal, possible explosion	10	Paint line low on paint	6	Automated inventory mgt system	Automated inventory mgt system	2	120	None	None
B			10	Spray nozzle partially plugged	9	Regular nozzle cleaning procedure	None	4	360	Keep nozzle path when not in used in water	New procedure instituted

Action results

ID	Severity	Occurrence	Detection	RPN
2.B	10	3	4	120

Current detection method when constructing FMEA process in-cooperates the poka-yoka technique.

Leadership

Poka Yoka can be considered one of the great tools inside jidoka Philoshy. Jidoka principle is the second pillar of Toyota production system, and it emphasize on building quality into the process not fixing quality. Bringing the line to halt to avoid passing quality issues to the next stage is an essential management principle in jidoka. Jidoka in cooperate the use of andon cords to discover errors and immediately take actions. The instructions about how to react and take decisions must be standardized. Leadership must be trained on how to react to problems and immediately fix them.

Unfortunately, companies invest on technologies mistakenly thinking that technology can prevent errors. Technology can only support people and systems to prevent errors when there are good management system and people are trained on problems solving and how to react immediately to abnormalities.

Andon

We talked about Andon a lot in the Jidoka book and in this series, when we explained the breakdown of Jidoka. Andon is a system that alerts people to problems before they happen, in order to make the process more efficient and prevent issues. In manufacturing, an andon is a system that tells managers, maintenance workers, and other employees about a problem with quality or the manufacturing process. But is this all that Andon being?

According Lean Enterprise Institute, Andon is a visual management tool that helps people quickly see how things are going in an area. It also lets them know if something goes wrong.

- An andon is a tool that can be used to show or signal something.
- Production status refers to the current situation of machines in operation.
- A problem that is not normal, like a machine stopping, something wrong with the quality, issues with tools, delays by workers, or not having enough materials.

"Required actions, like switching or replacing something. "

Organizations can use andon to show how many units they planned to produce compared to how many they actually produced.

A regular andon is a sign hung from the ceiling with numbers on it that represent different work areas or machines. A number will light up when either:

- Indicator to alert the user.
- A person can either pull a string or press a button.

The bright number makes the team leader react quickly. Colored lights on machines show if there is a problem (red) or if everything is operating normally (green). This is another kind of andon.

Andon and Fixed-Position Stop are Tools Used in Manufacturing to Help Improve Efficiency and Safety

The stop system that Toyota uses in its assembly lines is well-known and works very well. When an operator has a problem, they pull a rope. This makes the production line stop, but not right away. The line stops after the product gets to a certain spot. We try to fix the problem right away to get the line working again. But, if we can't fix it in time, the conveyor stops in one place.

If there was a problem with one operation, it would cause all other operations to stop. As a result, this could lead to mistakes made by the person operating it, like putting it together incorrectly. Instead, coming to a stop at the set position (the end of each workstation) will not cause any harm to the safety and quality of other workstation processes. In simple words, this method helps to reduce the amount of time wasted, while also making sure that any problems that arise are fixed and defects are not allowed to continue.

• • • •

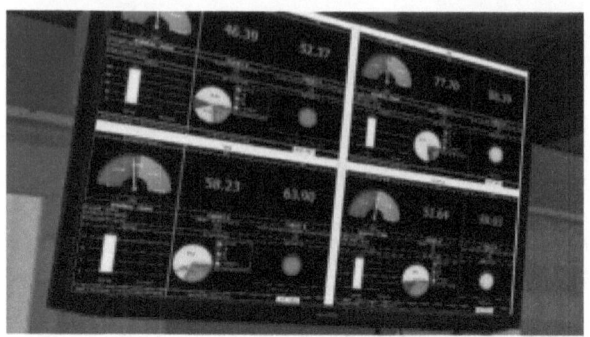

SOME COMPANIES USE special Andon device that helps workers see what is happening in the production system and alerts them to potential issues. It is usually a light-up sign placed above eye level in the production area.

We want to stress that Andon is a tool that shows problems, like quality issues or other problems. But the Japanese auto industry has been using it a lot to find and fix quality issues before they happen or get to the final product and are given to customers.

When it is used to show problems with how much is being produced compared to the goal, it helps leaders see the problems and start figuring out the main reasons behind them.

Goal:
Highest Quality, Lowest Cost, Shortest Lead Time
Best Safety, High Morale

Just In Time
Right part-
Right amount-
Right Time

·Flow
·Takt Time
·Pull
·Quick
Changeover

Culture

Flexible, Capable,
Highly Motivated
People

Jidoka
Quality at the
Source

·Line Stop
·Visual
Controls
·Error Proofing
·Andon
·5 Whys

Operational Stability
Standardized Work
PM/ TPM
5S
Leveled Production

Color	Status	Action
Green	Working	Proceed to next production step
Yellow	Problem appeared	Investigate problem and see if it needs production stop or can be fixed quickly without stopping production
Red	Production has Stopped	Production has stopped to fix the issue

Regretfully, there is a false misconception regarding the idea and how it functions, just like with many other businesses. When rival Toyota companies began to employ the andon system, they made the same error of thinking the line-stop system was hardwired to every single manufacturing line, as Liker demonstrated in The Toyota Way. Thus, pressing the button causes the entire assembly line to halt abruptly. The application of the andon principle is noticeably different at Toyota. An andon button, when pressed by an operator, causes the workstation to light up in yellow, much like a traffic light, but the line doesn't stop moving. Before the andon turns, the team leader has tilled the product goes into the next workstation zone to take action prior to the andon turning red and the line segment coming to an automatic halt. Liker clarified that on a Toyota assembly line producing automobiles at a time, this is probably going to take 15 to 30 seconds. The team leader has the option to either promptly resolve the issue or indicate that it can wait until the automobile passes other workstations and then press the button once again to reverse the line stoppage.

Alternatively, the team leader may decide that the line should end.

There are numerous things to think about and pointers provided in The Toyota Way for that system:

1. The team leader must also receive training on a standardizing approach for answering phone calls.

2. Small product buffers should be placed between each segment of the assembly line (a Toyota buffer normally consists of seven to ten automobiles). The buffer allows the following line to continue operating after a line segment stops for around ten minutes, at which point the plant as a whole shut down—which happens infrequently.

3. Andon aims to increase quality rather than decrease output. Toyota accomplished Andon's goal without needlessly risking lost output.

Andon and Gemba

B ecause andon is a part of the visualization program, it's a helpful tool for leaders and managers to quickly discover problems without interrupting the workers. Visualization is a significant apparatus for every day management and for supervisors and pioneers rehearsing gemba walks on daily basis. It enables a chief to see the present circumstance without intruding on the procedure, and it permits individuals who take the necessary steps to follow their own advance and respond to any inconstancy. This culture of surfacing issues requires a great deal of help from ranking directors and pioneers. Individuals should likewise be prepared for autonomous critical thinking to solve problems.

Visualization ought to be in every single operational zone for the shop floor. For instance, in the region of production, track hourly targets to take care of issues step by step and furthermore track quality. In the zone of logistics, track on-time deliveries (Soliman, 2016). Visualization is a decent method to introduce the gap between the present circumstance and the perfect circumstance. Visualization enables everybody to follow their own advancement, and it enables the administrators to respond step by step to varieties and issues. So as to follow progress and utilize visualization, visual boards should exhibit the accompanying: (a) the hourly objective, so everyone can check whether this is a positive or negative hour, (b) the standard technique, so everyone can perceive what the standard strategy is, (c) the issues, so everyone can check whether the laborers comprehend their fundamental issues, and (d) moves being made, so everyone can perceive what individuals are doing about these issues (Balle and Balle, 2010).

When a leader notices an issue with the process, he should ask the following questions:

- Is the standardized work chart accurate in its times?
- Is the takt correct?
- Is the operator following the steps in sequence?
- Is the operator following the steps in timing?
- Are all the key points being followed?

Andon and Why-Why

When Leaders discover a problem and begin asking questions, According to Sakichi Toyoda, who invented the method, "by repeating why five times, the nature of the problem as well as its solution becomes clear." The five whys are utilized to construct the specifics of a problem-solving strategy, while the five whys are used to delve further into an issue.

Don't forget these shop-floor courtesy:

- Bring your tools: A stopwatch, graph paper, pencil, eraser and calculator.
- Approach the process via the team leader and the supervisor.
- Introduce yourself, explain what you are doing, and don't interrupt operators while they are working.
- Explain that you are watching the work, not the operator.
- Show any notes you have taken.
- Say "thank you" before you leave.
- Keep hands out of pockets on the shop floor. People are working hard, and jamming your hands in your pockets sends a too casual message. A better message is, "We are all working hard for the customer."

Andon VS Poka-Yoke

Have you gotten the different? I hope so!

When I have a process for loading parts, I use devices called poka yoke to make sure the operator doesn't put the wrong part in, or put it in the wrong way, or put it in the wrong place before starting the process.

Poka yoka simply means anything that helps stop mistakes or problems from happening in a process. Poka Yoke can be used to make products, processes, or systems better. It comes in three types: prevention, detection, and correction. Poka Yoke's purpose is to reduce or get rid of the need for checking and fixing mistakes, and to make sure things are done right the first time.

Andon is a system that allows the operator to get help if something goes wrong during a process. They can press a button to call for help from a manager or maintenance person. If the worker in charge of fixing things is not close by, they can check the andon board to see where they need to go.

Andon is a light (visual) or sound (audible) that tells workers and managers about a problem in a process. A person or a machine can start it if they notice a problem. The reason for Andon is to stop the work, find out why there's a problem, and fix it so it doesn't happen again.

How Andon and Poka Yoke Work Together?

It's clear that Andon and Poka Yoke are different in terms of their focus and timing. Andon focuses on detecting and resolving problems that have already occurred, while Poka Yoke focuses on preventing or minimizing problems from occurring in the first place. Andon is activated after a problem is detected, while Poka Yoke is implemented before a problem can occur.

Andon and Poka Yoke are tools that work together to make things better all the time. They both help to cut down on waste, make things better, and make customers happier. Andon and Poka Yoke can help each other by giving feedback. Andon signals tell us about problems, and Poka Yoke helps to fix or stop these problems from happening again. By using Andon and Poka Yoke together, you can help your team solve problems, learn, and be more creative in your organization.

It's important to set clear rules for how things should be done and let everyone know about them so that Andon and Poka Yoke can work well. It's important to teach employees how to use Andon and Poka Yoke, and to set up and take care of devices and methods used in the work. Also, we need to gather and study information from Andon signals and Poka Yoke solutions to find the main reasons for problems, take action to fix them, and check if the solutions worked. Regularly, we should check and change the rules, systems, and ways to make things better. We should also share what we have learned with our team and organization.

Using Andon and Poka Yoke together can help you make better products and work more efficiently. It can reduce mistakes and waste in your work, making things better overall. This could also make customers happier and more likely to keep coming back by giving them good products and services that they really like. Also, we can make work safer and make workers feel happier and more involved by making sure they feel less stressed, less frustrated and less bored. We can also do this by giving them more freedom, more responsibility and more recognition. Finally, it can help make a workplace where people are always trying to make things better and solve problems for customers and stakeholders.

Appendix: Jidoka - Building Culture of Stopping the Production Line

I first learned about Jidoka when I worked for a manufacturing company in Egypt. They wanted to use Jidoka to make their products better and safer. In this factory, if you didn't work at full capacity for the entire shift, you had to give a reason to the different departments. We prioritize quantity over quality and regular maintenance. By developing a habit of addressing and solving problems, you are motivating employees to not keep their issues hidden. These issues can significantly impact profits and efficiency. You need to think ahead and make plans to be productive for a long time.

The old way of thinking about productivity was to make lots of parts using as much resources and machines as possible, so that each part would be cheaper to produce. This approach believes that when more products are made, the cost per unit becomes lower. If any problem comes up, we can deal with it later because we have a lot of extra supplies that will keep things running smoothly even if there are issues. Problems are not logical or reasonable. In large-scale production, quality is checked again through inspection. Also, if you are making 500 parts and there is a problem with how they are made, all of those parts may end up being faulty. The losses will be very big. There are also hidden problems, and it will be very difficult to find out where the mistake is coming from. So, the main reasons will stay unknown.

With lean, production is done one step at a time. If one step stops, everything else stops and there is a feeling of needing to hurry. Now everyone knows that we have some problems that need to be solved. We need to work on finding a permanent solution to these problems, or else there will be too many instances of work being halted.

How does Jidoka stop quality issues from happening?

Jidoka's main aim is to avoid any problems with quality from going into the next step or reaching the customer, which can be really bad. This is one of the great advantages of lean, which works hard to reduce the number of items produced at once. At the same time, Toyota wants to make sure they continue making cars without any interruptions or risks to the production process. That's why they made a system called "Minimizing Line Stoppage Time" which uses techniques to solve problems and prevent mistakes. Dr Liker explained how the problem-solving cycle is connected to the Jidoka culture in his book called Toyota Way Field.

1. Identifying problems: standardization is important for ensuring quality. It is hard to tell if there is a problem or not without a standard. If there are no rules, people will do things in their own way, which can lead to problems with the quality of work. Standard work is a way to compare things. If the person in charge notices a problem, they should fix it right away. If there is a problem that cannot be solved, the person in charge must ask for assistance.

2. Escalation: The concept of artificial intelligence (AI) is advancing rapidly. AI refers to a technology that allows machines to perform tasks that normally require human intelligence, such as visual perception, speech recognition, and decision-making. This technology has the potential to greatly impact various industries, including healthcare, finance, and transportation. However, there are concerns about the ethical

implications of AI and how it could affect job opportunities for humans. Despite these concerns, AI continues to develop and has the potential to revolutionize many aspects of our lives. Increasing problems: If the situation is getting worse or the problem is not small, the employee should ask for help. When you pull the cord, it signals that you need help. The andon instrument used by Toyota sends signals fast to the assigned support people, like Toyota team leaders and group leaders. This usually includes a loud noise and a light that shows where something is.

3. Estimate: the leader needs to fix the issue in a certain amount of time. If he couldn't do this, he needs to tell someone higher up. Afterwards, the leaders need to find solutions to these problems and make sure they don't happen again. The management's job is to make sure that the things needed for work are given to everyone in a clear way.

4. Control: The person in charge needs to address the root cause of problems. Go through the line and solve the problems forever. If we can't figure out what is causing the problem, the leaders need to decide to start over again.

5. Eliminating root causes: once the problem is under control and work is back on track, the team needs to figure out where the differences are coming from. They will use a method called PDCA to find the best solution to prevent the problem from happening again and causing another halt in production.

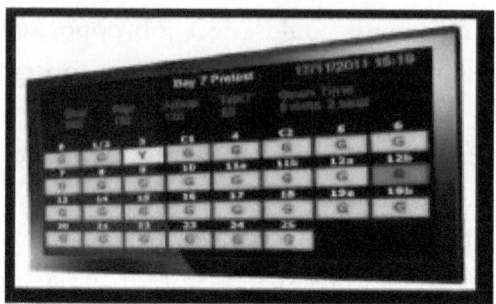

Jidoka is a Principle That Focuses on Making High-Quality Products without Sacrificing the Production speed.

U nfortunately, and like many other companies there is a wrong misunderstand about the concept and how it operates. As Liker illustrated in The Toyota Way when Toyota competitors started to use the andon system, they made the same mistake of assuming the line-stop system was hardwired to each and every production line. So, when the button is pushed, the entire assembly line like comes to a screeching halt. At Toyota, the principle of andon is worked remarkably different. When an operator in a workstation pushes an andon button, that workstation will light up in yellow typically like the traffic light, but the line will continue moving. The team leader has until the product moves into the next workstation zone to respond, before the andon turns red and the line segment automatically stop. As Liker explained, in Toyota this likely is to be a matter of 15-30 seconds on an assembly line making cars at one minute. In that time the team leader might immediately fix the problem or note it can be fixed while the car is moving into other workstations and push the button again, canceling out the line stoppage. Or the team leader might conclude the line should stop.

In that system, that are many considerations and tips presented in The Toyota Way:

1. The team leader has to be trained as well on a standardization procedure on how to respond to andon calls.

2. The assembly line should be divided into segments with small buffers of products in between (in Toyota this buffer is typically 7-10 cars). Because of the buffer, when a line segment stops, the next line can keep working for about 10 minutes using the buffer and before the entire plant is shut down and rarely does it do shutdown.

3. The purpose of andon is to build in quality, not to lose production. Toyota achieved the purpose of andon without taking needless risks of lost production.

4. Some manufacturers assign a worker to watch the machine for error. This is a waste of the human precise time! Operator that is watching the machine for error is a pure waste and you have to develop a method (like Toyota andon) so problems are surfaced automatically when they occur.

The Two Distinct Interpretations of the Jidoka Principle

The first concept is to separate man from machine. It was normal in the original parent company for a single young woman to operate many machines since they were automated. So, when Mr. Ohno came to the automotive company after WW II and saw one man operating one machine tool, he thought that it was strange and inefficient.

He embarked upon a path of breaking down the notion of one man one machine in the engine shops. Instead of "monitoring" machines the operator was to walk between two machine tools and keep them both up and running. Then three machines and four machines and so on.

The second concept of Jidoka is of course the concept of building in 100% quality every time at the process and not inspecting it in later downstream.

This means you have to have a highly capable process and know how to maintain all the key variables in the process so that a good part is made every time. If a problem occurs the machine should stop right away.

The main purpose of Jidoka principle is to discover quality problems at earlier stages, find the root causes and eliminate the problem from recurring again in the future. By doing so you are saving both your customer and your business. If a defected product is passed to customer so this is a problem and because customers are what keep you in business, you have to build quality for them. This is one of the main lean goals. The goal is to prevent a quality issue that is reducing productivity every day and killing your capacity, decreasing value, increasing costs and reducing safety. Lean encourages you to make it right from first time and this is why surfacing problems is important and can't be done without a single-piece-flow system. Inspecting defects before they pass to the customer is not really the main goal of lean. But having a system that allow information to flow, problems to surface so they can be fixed immediately is the goal. Root causes should be identified and eliminated through kaizen. With lean, there is no or very little inventory buffer, so when process A stops process B will stop too. This allow problems to be noticed quickly and eliminated. There will be no more underlying costs and hidden wastes.

You can't compromise quality. Quality problems are one of the greatest wastes in the process. Quality is what adds value for your customer and keeps you in business and defective products that reach the customer can lead to complete business loss.

Examining Quality Defects to Remove the Causes

B asically, it is easy to keep track of the number of faulty products produced using just a piece of paper. It is difficult to know what caused the defects. Understanding the reason behind the quality problem can be difficult and it may take a lot of effort. This is why doing one task at a time improves the quality of work. When you see problems early, you can fix them right away before they become big and expensive.

Identifying issues with quality is a crucial task for managers. When practitioners have problems, they often use a complicated method called Six Sigma to figure out what is causing the differences. However, frequently just going and observing (called gemba) can help easily identify the true cause. Watching the operator do their job, checking if it meets the standards, and getting the technical team involved can help solve many issues. Comparing the machine or process with another one that makes the same part with fewer mistakes can make the analysis even faster and simpler.

At Toyota, managers don't use many complicated statistical tools for quality. In simpler terms, they usually use methods like going to see for themselves, using techniques to prevent mistakes, using a simple analysis tool called Pareto, and problem-solving methods like asking "why" five times. This information can be found in a popular book called The Toyota Way.

Methods used to make things better

There are many tools to help achieve quality goals in every part of the process. There are lots of tools that can help you avoid quality issues before they happen and help you make a product without any mistakes. Poka Yoka, a Japanese term also known as mistake-proofing, is a helpful tool for stopping human errors. I have used it many times myself when evaluating the causes and effects of failures. This tool can make things better in many different types of businesses like services, making things, and designing things. Inventory control is a method that is typically connected to any device that prevents mistakes.

There are many real-world applications where mistake-proofing is used in product design. Here are some examples to make sure things are done correctly: limit switches to check that a part is in the right place or fixture before it is worked on; part features that only allow assembly in the correct way; special connectors to prevent mistakenly connecting wire harnesses or cables incorrectly; part symmetry that prevents wrong insertion.

Sadly, some companies mistakenly believe that investing in technology will prevent mistakes. Technology can only help people and systems avoid mistakes if there is a good management system in place and people are trained to solve problems and respond quickly to problems.

To figure out why a product doesn't work and what needs to be done to prevent it from happening again, you can use a technique called failure mode and effect analysis.

Failure mode effect analysis (FMEA) is a way to evaluate how likely something is to fail, how bad the failure would be, and how easy it would be to recognize the failure. If we have more ways to find and anticipate problems, the chances of something going wrong with the product are reduced. FMEA is a useful tool for improving quality if used correctly. I wrote an article for the Industrial Management magazine called "Analyzing Failure to Prevent Problems. " A lot of organizations only use FMEA when they are making something, but FMEA can also be used when they are fixing something or taking care of it.

Lean is not a set of tools used in manufacturing to reduce expenses and increase profits. Lean is a way to make customers happy by giving them higher quality things while also charging them less. Creating a product that solves the problems your customers face when using it is a valid goal for lean engineering. Lean is about coming up with new and creative ideas. If you can make a product without any flaws or include good quality in the design, it will make customers happy and increase their trust.

Toyota Under Fire book is a closer look at how important it is to have a strong culture that can support you when things go wrong. The talks about why Toyota does what it does were really useful. This shows that the decisions made before the crisis are the most important ones. And then, when there is a crisis, go back to the fundamentals. Explore and expand more extensively.

References:

Ahmed, M. H. (2013). Lean transformation guidance: Why organizations fail to achieve and sustain excellence through lean improvement. International Journal of Lean Thinking, 4(1), 31–40.

Ahmed, M. H. (2014). Daily walks train future leaders. Industrial Management, 56(1), 22–27.

Byrne, A. 2012. Lean Turnaround: The Lean Turnaround: How Business Leaders Use Lean Principles to Create Value and Transform Their Company. McGraw-Hill Educations.

Liker, J. K. 2003. The Toyota Way: 14 Management Principles from the World's Greatest Manufacturer. New York: McGraw-Hill.

Liker, J. K., and D. Meier. 2005. The Toyota Way Fieldbook: A Practical Guide for Implementing Toyota's 4Ps. New York: McGraw-Hill.

Womack, J. P., and Jones, D.T. (1996). Lean Thinking: Banish Waste and Create Wealth in Your Corporation. Free Press.

Liker, J. K., and T. N. Ogden. 2010. Toyota Under Fire: Lessons for Turning Crisis into Opportunity. New York: McGraw-Hill.

Liker, J.K. The Toyota Way: 14 Management Principles from the World's Greatest Manufacturer. McGraw-Hill Educations.

Rother, M. 2009. The Toyota Kata: Managing People for Improvement, Adaptiveness and Superior Results. New York: McGraw-Hill.

Rother, M., Harris, R. 2001. Creating Continuous Flow: Creating Continuous Flow: An Action Guide for Managers, Engineers & Production Associates. Lean Enterprise Institute Publications.

Soliman, M. H. A. (2015b). What Toyota production system is really about? (Unpublished).

Soliman, M. H. A. (2016). Hoshin Kanri: How Toyota creates a culture of continuous improvement to achieve lean goals. CreateSpace.

Soliman, M. H. A. (2015). A new routine for culture change. Industrial Management, 57(3), 25–30.

Soliman, M., A Comprehensive Review of Manufacturing Wastes: Toyota Production System Lean Principles, 2017.

Soliman, M. H. A. (2020). Takt Time, Cycle Time, One-Piece Flow, and Heijunka.

Soliman, M. H. A. (2020). Kanban the Toyota Way: An Inventory Buffering System to Eliminate Inventory. KDP.

Soliman, M. H. A. (2017). Why continuous improvement programs fail in the Egyptian manufacturing organizations: A research study of the evidence. American Journal of Industrial and Business Management, 7(3), 202–222. https://doi.org/10.4236/ajibm.2017.73016

Soliman, M. H. A. (2016). Hoshin Kanri: How Toyota creates a culture of continuous improvement to achieve lean goals. CreateSpace.

Soliman, M. H. A. (2020). Gemba Walks the Toyota Way: The Place to Teach and Learn Management. KDP.

Soliman, M. H. A. (2020). Jidoka - The Missing Pillar!

Soliman, M. H. A. (2020). Jidoka: The Toyota Principle of Building Quality into the Process. KDP.

Soliman, M. H. A. 2014. "Analyzing Failure to Prevent Problems." Industrial Management 56 (5): 10.

Soliman, M. H. A. 2013. OEE Can Be Your Key: Change Formula for Equipment Availability to Improve Performance. Industrial Engineer 45 (8): 43.

Don't miss out!

Visit the website below and you can sign up to receive emails whenever Mohammed Hamed Ahmed Soliman publishes a new book. There's no charge and no obligation.

https://books2read.com/r/B-A-VCQM-DTHQC

BOOKS 2 READ

Connecting independent readers to independent writers.

Did you love *Poka Yoke - Design for Great Quality*? Then you should read *The Guidebook to Toyota's 13 Pillars System - Series Books 7 to 17* by Mohammed Hamed Ahmed Soliman!

Toyota Motor Corporation created a production system that aims to achieve high-quality products, minimize expenses, and shorten the time it takes to make them by reducing waste. TPS consists of two main components, just-in-time and jidoka, and is usually represented by the "house" image shown on the right. To make TPS better and keep it working well, we follow a process called PDCA or the scientific method. We do this by repeatedly doing standardized work and making small improvements called kaizen.The development of TPS is attributed to Taiichi Ohno, who was in charge of production at Toyota after World War II.

Ohno started implementing TPS at Toyota in the 1950s and 1960s, beginning with machining operations. He then expanded its use to other areas within the company and shared it with other suppliers during the 1960s and 1970s. Outside of Japan, spreading started in a serious way when Toyota and General Motors created a partnership called NUMMI in California in 1984.The ideas of just-in-time (JIT) and jidoka were developed before the war. Sakichi Toyoda, who started the Toyota group of companies, came up with the idea of jidoka a long time ago. He did this by adding a device to his automatic looms that would make the loom stop if a thread broke. This made things a lot better in terms of quality and allowed people to focus on more important work instead of just watching machines for quality. Over time, this simple idea became a part of every machine, every production line, and every Toyota operation.Kiichiro Toyoda, the son of Sakichi and the person who started the Toyota car company, came up with the idea of JIT (Just-in-Time) in the 1930s. He ordered that Toyota should not have too much extra inventory and that Toyota will try to work together with suppliers to have a consistent production level. Ohno led the development of JIT, a special system to manage production and control overproduction.TPS became well-known when The Machine That Changed the World was published in 1990. This book was the result of five years of research led by the Massachusetts Institute of Technology. The scientists at MIT discovered that TPS was much better and faster than traditional mass production. It was such a big change that they called it lean production to show how different it was.

Read more at https://www.personal-lean.org/.

Also by Mohammed Hamed Ahmed Soliman

How to Develop Mission, Strategy, Goals and Values That Fit with Company's Vision Statement
Lean Approach to Cost-Benefit Analysis
Genchi Genbutsu Process – The Role of Gemba in Lean Management and Value Creation
Toyota's Approach to Developing and Coaching Leaders
How to Create Continuous Production Flow?
Lean Culture - How Toyota Encourages Employees to Embrace Lean Behaviors and Practices
5S- The True Mean to Enhance Productivity and Work Value for Customers
Understanding the Toyota Production System's Genetics
The Guidebook to Toyota's 13 Pillars System - Series Books 7 to 17
The Guidebook to Toyota's Corporate Strategy and Leadership – Series Books 1 to 6
What are The Improvement Kata and Coaching Kata?
Process Mapping the Toyota Way
Application of Lean in Non-manufacturing Environments - Series Books 18 to 19

Standalone

Hoshin Kanri: How Toyota Creates a Culture of Continuous Improvement to Achieve Lean Goals
The Seven Deadly Wastes and How to Remove Them from Your Business: The Heart of the Toyota Production System
Overall Equipment Effectiveness Simplified: Analyzing OEE to find the Improvement Opportunities

Machinery Oil Analysis & Condition Monitoring : A Practical Guide to Sampling and Analyzing Oil to Improve Equipment Reliability

Practical Guide to FMEA : A Proactive Approach to Failure Analysis

Industrial Applications of Infrared Thermography: How Infrared Analysis Can be Used to Improve Equipment Inspection

Ultrasound Analysis for Condition Monitoring: Applications of Ultrasound Detection for Various Industrial Equipment

Brainstorming for Problems Solving: How Leaders Can Achieve a Successful Brainstorming Session

Vibration Basics and Machine Reliability Simplified : A Practical Guide to Vibration Analysis

Gemba Walks the Toyota Way : The Place to Teach and Learn Management

Jidoka: The Toyota Principle of Building Quality into the Process

Turning PDCA into a Routine for Learning

Toyota Healthcare: 7+1 Types Of Waste

Kanban the Toyota Way: An Inventory Buffering System to Eliminate Inventory

Takt Time: A Guide to the Very Basic Lean Calculation

5S: A Practical Guide to Visualizing and Organizing Workplaces to Improve Productivity

Machine Reliability and Condition Monitoring: A Comprehensive Guide to Predictive Maintenance Planning

The Ultimate Guide to Successful Lean Transformation: Top Reasons Why Companies Fail to Achieve and Sustain Excellence through Lean Improvement

Toyota Standard Work: The Foundation of Kaizen

Watch for more at https://www.personal-lean.org/.

About the Author

Mohammed Hamed Ahmed Soliman is an industrial engineer, consultant, university lecturer, operational excellence leader, and author. He works as a lecturer at the American University in Cairo and as a consultant for several international industrial organizations.

Soliman earned a Bachelor's of science in Engineering and a Master's degree in Quality Management. He earned post-graduate degrees in Industrial Engineering and Engineering Management. He holds numerous certificates in management, industry, quality, and cost engineering.

For most of his career, Soliman worked as a regular employee for various industrial sectors. This included crystal-glass making, fertilizers, and chemicals. He did this while educating people about the culture of continuous improvement. Soliman has more than 15 years of experience and proven track record of achieving high levels of operational excellence to a broad range of business operations including manufacturing, service and healthcare. He has led several improvement projects within leading organizations and defined a lot of savings in the manufacturing wastes stream.

Soliman has lectured at Princess Noura University and trained the maintenance team in Vale Oman Pelletizing Company. He has been lecturing at The American University in Cairo for 8 years and has designed and delivered 40 leadership and technical skills enhancement training modules. In the past 4 years, Soliman's lectures have been popular and attracted a large audience of over 200,000 people according to SlideShare's analysis.. His research is one of the most downloaded works on the Social Science Research Network, which is run by ELSEVIER. His research is one of the most downloaded works on the Social Science Research Network, which is run by ELSEVIER.

Soliman is a senior member at the Institute of Industrial and Systems Engineers and a member with the Society for Engineering and Management Systems. He has published more than 60 publications including articles in peer reviewed academic journals and international magazines. His writings on lean manufacturing, leadership, productivity, and business appear in Industrial Engineers, Lean Thinking, Industrial Management, and Sage Publications. Soliman's blog is www.personal-lean.org.

Read more at https://www.personal-lean.org/.

About the Publisher

Personal-lean is dedicated to publish high quality educational content, assessment, training in the filed of business for various industrial sectors. And is a growing educational organization, with products and services in various countries.